"I will hang onto this book in the hope that I can some day read it to my grandchildren."
TIM CHALLIES, author and blogger

"Why didn't someone write this book decades ago? A gentle and delightful introduction to a crucial topic."
JONATHAN LEEMAN, author and father of four

"God made Trillia write this book, and that was a very good idea!
Young and old alike should read this story often."
KRISTIE ANYABWILE, pastor's wife, mom, Bible teacher, writer

"As a mom of six young bi-racial sons, I'm so very grateful for Trillia's beautiful and
joy-filled account of God's design and purpose in creating us all uniquely."
RUTH CHOU SIMONS, artist and author of *GraceLaced*; founder of gracelaced.com

"God-centered, clear, and helpful. I highly recommend this book."
BLAIR LINNE, spoken-word artist

"This book is a treasure and a joy for our family."
AARON AND JAMIE IVEY, musician, and host of *The Happy Hour with Jamie Ivey* podcast

"Touching and beautiful, this will engage kids and their parents too!"
NANCY GUTHRIE, Bible teacher and author

"Compelling and captivating."
CHAMP THORNTON, author of *The Radical Book for Kids*

"What a great resource to share with the next generation."
GLORIA FURMAN, author of *Missional Motherhood* and *Alive in Him*

"A delight. Cuddle up with a little one and share the news of God's very good idea."
MELISSA KRUGER, author of *Walking with God in the Season of Motherhood*

thegoodbook
for children

God's Very Good Idea
© Trillia Newbell / Catalina Echeverri / The Good Book Company 2017.
Reprinted 2018 (four times), 2019, 2020 (four times).

Illustrated by Catalina Echeverri | Design & Art Direction by André Parker

"The Good Book For Children" is an imprint of The Good Book Company Ltd.
thegoodbook.com | thegoodbook.co.uk
thegoodbook.com.au | thegoodbook.co.nz | thegoodbook.co.in

ISBN: 9781784982218 | Printed in Turkey

WRITTEN BY

Trillia Newbell

God's very good idea

ILLUSTRATED BY

Catalina Echeverri

A TRUE STORY ABOUT GOD'S DELIGHTFULLY DIFFERENT FAMILY

In the beginning — in fact, before the beginning — God had...

It was an even better idea than...

Solar panels, 1954

Chocolate chip cookies, 1938

The Super Soaker, 1982

Color TV, 1942

Fireworks, 700 BC

Roller skates, 1760

The lifecraft, 1880

The X-ray machine, 1895

God's idea was to make PEOPLE...
lots of people... lots of different people...
who would all enjoy loving him and
all enjoy loving each other.

They would all be made in his image. They would all be like mirrors, reflecting what God is like.

Because God is full of love, they would be full of love too.

So God got to work. He **MADE** a beautiful world for people to live in. Then he made the first people — a man and a woman.

And he said to them:

"Be happy. Enjoy loving me and loving each other. Have a huge family that will fill the earth and look after the earth and enjoy the earth."

All of them were
made in his image.

God carried on
creating people.

And all of them
were different too.

Some were men,

and some
were women.

Some liked reading,

Some had
darker skin,

and some had
lighter skin.

and some liked
riding bikes.

Some had curly
hair, and some had
straight hair.

We live in God's world. We are all different, but we are also all the same. Everyone you see is different than you, and the same as you. They might look different or speak different or play different. But they are all made in God's image, and so they are all valuable.

This is God's
very good idea. But...

People **RUINED** God's very good idea.

The first people chose not to love God.
This is called sin. And because they chose
not to love God as they should, they forgot
how to love each other as they should.

We are the same. We choose not to love God, and so we are not able to love each other like we should. We sin. Sometimes we treat others badly because they are different than us.

People fight with each other.
People are mean to each other.
People laugh at each other.

Because we have ruined God's very good idea, he is not pleased with us. Our sin means we can't be friends with him, or enjoy living with him.

We need God's forgiveness for ruining his very good idea. It's the same for everyone in the world.

People who like reading need forgiveness, and people who like riding bikes need forgiveness.

People with darker skin need forgiveness, and people with lighter skin need forgiveness.

People with curly hair need forgiveness, and people with straight hair need forgiveness.

But God was not surprised by people ruining things. He had always had a very good plan to **RESCUE** his very good idea.

So God got
to work.

He came to earth as a person — JESUS.

Jesus loved people who were different than him. He loved peopl who no one else loved.

I CAN SEE!

He always enjoyed loving all the different people he met. Jesus shows us how to enjoy loving each other.

But people didn't love Jesus.
Instead, they hated him.

They put him on a
cross to die. But this
was part of God's plan.

On the cross, Jesus took
our sin so that we can
be forgiven.

Jesus forgives his people
for their sins.

Jesus didn't stay dead. He rose
back to life and then went
back to live in heaven.

And then he gave people his
Spirit, to help them enjoy
loving him and loving all the
different people they know.

Jesus helps us to love each other.

One day, God will FINISH his very good idea. Jesus will come back and make the world perfect again. And anyone who has asked Jesus to forgive them will live there, with their different languages and skin colors.

They will enjoy loving God and loving each other. They will enjoy praising God for making, rescuing and finishing his very good idea.

But here's a very, very, very good part of God's very good idea. You don't have to wait till then to enjoy it!

Jesus welcomes anyone who asks him to forgive them. And when Jesus welcomes someone, he welcomes them into his family forever.

He welcomes people who like reading, and people who like riding bikes.

He welcomes people with darker skin, and people with lighter skin.
He welcomes people with curly hair, and people with straight hair.

God's family is called the church.
Your church friends are your brothers
and sisters — your wonderful and colorful
church family. You can enjoy loving them
and loving God with them.

This is God's very good idea:
lots of different people enjoying
loving him and loving each other.

God **MADE** it.
People **RUINED** it.
He **RESCUED** it.
He will **FINISH** it.

And, with your church family, you can
enjoy being part of it right now!

HOW DO WE KNOW
ABOUT GOD'S VERY GOOD IDEA?

The story in this book begins where all things begin, in Genesis 1.
In the beginning, "God created mankind in his own image ... male and female"
(Genesis 1 v 27). And "God blessed them" (v 28). Part of living a blessed life is
to enjoy loving God and loving each other in his world.

Every man and woman ever born is created in the image of God. Every
tribe, tongue, and nation has the privilege of being a part of this magnificent
distinction. As God's image-bearers we are all equal in dignity and worth—but
we are all also equally fallen (Romans 3 v 23). This is why it is wonderful that
Jesus came to rescue people from every tribe, tongue, and nation. One day there
will be "a great multitude that no one [can] count, from every nation, tribe, people
and language, standing before the throne," praising God (Revelation 7 v 9-10).

This understanding—that God has created each of us equally with
dignity, value, and beauty—should inform our views of one another. Knowing
that we're made in his image and that he loves us enough
to want to forgive us means we can, with his Spirit's help,
truly love one another.